Contents

Introduction

As you grow up, you go through all sorts of changes. Physically your body changes from that of a child to that of a young adult, and looks and feels very different. Your emotions may, at times, feel as if they are all over the place. People's expectations of you also change. Parents, school, the community you live in and society in general give you more rights and responsibilities. At the same time they expect you to show maturity, proving that you can handle and value the rights and responsibilities you have been given.

In this book we are going to look at these changes. There's information on physical changes, on how you can best take care of your body, and on your rights and responsibilities. The book explores some of the difficulties you may face and suggests ways of coping with them.

What is health?

What does health mean to you?

- Eating the right foods?
- Getting plenty of exercise and rest?
- Taking care of your personal hygiene?

But is this really all that being healthy is about? Surely there are other health-related issues to think about...

- How you feel about yourself.
- Coping with and understanding all the changes that happen to your body during **puberty** and learning to recognize and handle all the emotions that fly around during this period of growing up!
- Coping with the times of hassle and conflict at school, home or with friends, and all the related stresses.
- Learning to handle your rights and understanding your responsibilities to yourself and others.
- Learning to deal with 'intimate' relationships.

FACT

95% of women try weight loss diets, only 5% of these diets are successful.

HEALTH & YOU

Julie Johnson

Heinemann
LIBRARY

www.heinemann.co.uk
Visit our website to find out more information about **Heinemann Library** books.

To order:
 Phone 44 (0) 1865 888066
 Send a fax to 44 (0) 1865 314091
Visit the Heinemann Bookshop at www.heinemann.co.uk to browse our catalogue
and order online.

First published in Great Britain by Heinemann Library, Halley Court, Jordan Hill, Oxford OX2 8EJ,
a division of Reed Educational and Professional Publishing Ltd.
Heinemann is a registered trademark of Reed Educational & Professional Publishing Limited.

OXFORD MELBOURNE AUCKLAND
JOHANNESBURG BLANTYRE GABORONE
IBADAN PORTSMOUTH NH (USA) CHICAGO

Designed by Tinstar Design (www.tinstar.co.uk)
Illustrations by Oxford Illustrators
Originated by Ambassador Litho Ltd
Printed by Wing King Tong in Hong Kong

ISBN ISBN 0 431 03532 6 (hardback)   ISBN 0 431 03537 7 (paperback)
04 03 02 01 00   04 03 02 01 00
10 9 8 7 6 5 4 3 2   10 9 8 7 6 5 4 3 2 1

British Library Cataloguing in Publication Data

Johnson, Julie
        Health and you. – (What's at issue)
        1. Health – Juvenile literature 2. Teenagers – Health and hygiene –
        Juvenile literature
        I. Title
        613 ' .0433

Acknowledgements

The Publishers would like to thank the following for permission to reproduce photographs: Advertising Archives p30;
Bubbles/ Pauline Cutler pp 6, 23(t), 36, 37,/David Lane p 29(b); Trevor Clifford pp 4–5, 8, 9(l), 21, 38, 41; Sally
Greenhill p 23(b); Rex Features/Nils Jurgensen pp 9(r), 10; The Stockmarket/Paul Barton p 24; Tony Stone Images/
Peter Cade pp 18, 31,/Howard Grey p 34,/Charles Thatcher p 32,/Bill Truslow p 26; Trip & Ast Directors/ Menneer
p 29(t).

Cover photograph reproduced with permission of Trevor Clifford Photography.

Our thanks to Julie Turner (School Counsellor, Banbury School, Oxfordshire) for her comments in the preparation of
this book.

Every effort has been made to contact copyright holders of any material reproduced in this book.
Any omissions will be rectified in subsequent printings if notice is given to the Publisher.

Any words appearing in the text in bold, **like this**, are explained in the Glossary.

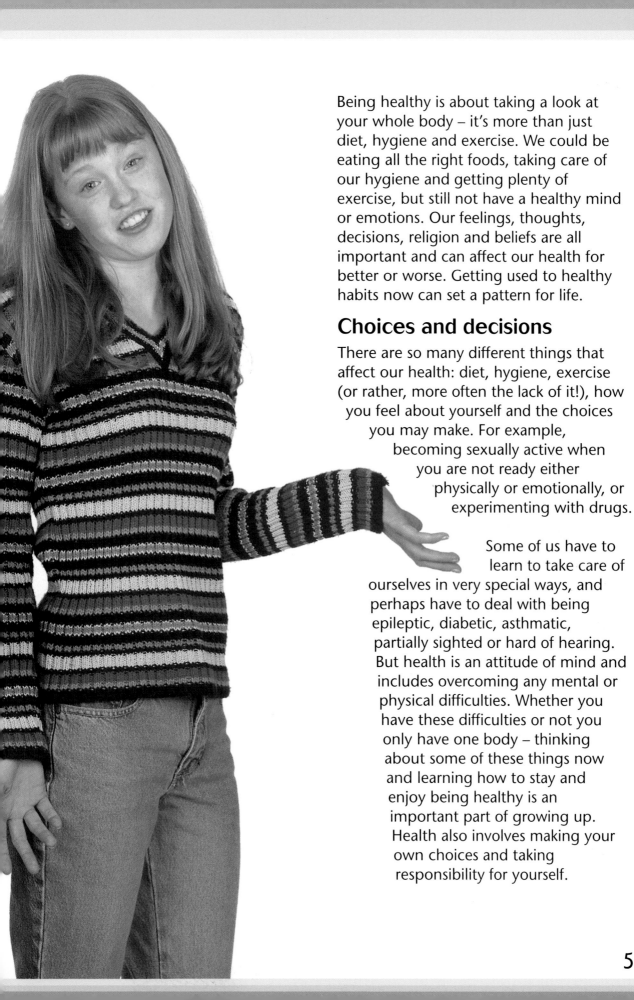

Being healthy is about taking a look at your whole body – it's more than just diet, hygiene and exercise. We could be eating all the right foods, taking care of our hygiene and getting plenty of exercise, but still not have a healthy mind or emotions. Our feelings, thoughts, decisions, religion and beliefs are all important and can affect our health for better or worse. Getting used to healthy habits now can set a pattern for life.

Choices and decisions

There are so many different things that affect our health: diet, hygiene, exercise (or rather, more often the lack of it!), how you feel about yourself and the choices you may make. For example, becoming sexually active when you are not ready either physically or emotionally, or experimenting with drugs.

Some of us have to learn to take care of ourselves in very special ways, and perhaps have to deal with being epileptic, diabetic, asthmatic, partially sighted or hard of hearing. But health is an attitude of mind and includes overcoming any mental or physical difficulties. Whether you have these difficulties or not you only have one body – thinking about some of these things now and learning how to stay and enjoy being healthy is an important part of growing up. Health also involves making your own choices and taking responsibility for yourself.

Taking care of yourself

Over the next few years your body will be changing a great deal – how much do you know about taking care of yourself? You only have one body and it will not take care of itself. Keeping your body clean, choosing the right foods, and getting enough exercise and rest will help you to stay fit and healthy.

'YOU ARE WHAT YOU EAT'

This old saying makes sense if you:
- eat a well balanced diet
- avoid fatty and sugary foods
- eat five portions of fruit or vegetables a day
- drink an average of 1.5 litres of water a day
- have breakfast, which is the most important meal of the day.

Following these tips, along with plenty of exercise, will keep you fit and healthy.

Yeah, but my parents are always on at me about eating proper meals.

I just love chips.

It is such a bore to think of healthy food.

The facts

Our bodies naturally perspire, or sweat, as a way of controlling body temperature. If perspiration is unable to evaporate and stays on your skin, then, after a while the normal **bacteria** on your skin will begin to react with it. This causes a rather unpleasant odour, more commonly known as body odour! Daily washing gets rid of the old sweat, so it is a good idea to have either a bath or shower every day. A shower or bath is especially important after doing any sporting activity. However, remember that just washing your body is not enough, don't forget to put on clean clothes!

Body odour

Body odour, or 'BO', is not only unpleasant for you, it will not be appreciated by those around you either! It can even lead to teasing and bullying. Some people are not always aware of their own body odour, so make sure you use large amounts of tact and sensitivity when letting someone know they have a problem with body odour.

You cannot prevent perspiration. It is a normal and important process – but you can use a deodorant under your arms. This can help keep you feeling and smelling fresh. Beware of the deodorants that are heavily perfumed – they can irritate sensitive skin. Lots of brands today are fragrance free. Avoid spray-on deodorants and use roll-on ones instead, these are healthier for young developing bodies and the environment too.

Say cheese!

You may have been born with two sets of teeth, but by now you will be on your second set. Your teeth will have to last you for the next 60 to 70 years at least, unless you don't mind having false teeth later in life and have plenty of money to buy them. Tooth decay and gum disease are the most common dental problems. Gum disease is one of the most common diseases in the world and a major reason why people lose healthy teeth, yet it is one of the easiest to prevent. It really is all down to you.

CHECK LIST FOR BEATING THE BUGS

- Regularly wash your body all over to keep your skin clean. Washing is especially important after taking exercise.
- Wash your face to keep those spots at bay.
- Brush your teeth and gums morning and night.
- Wash your hands after going to the toilet.
- Wash your hands before and after handling food.

HOW TO PREVENT TOOTH DECAY AND GUM DISEASE

- Brush teeth and gums twice a day (for at least two minutes each time).
- Avoid sugary foods.
- Drink water rather than sugary or fizzy drinks (even sugar-free fizzy drinks can damage teeth).
- Visit the dentist every six months.
- Change your toothbrush every two months.
- Use dental floss daily. (Ask your dentist how to use it if you are unsure).

Hair affair

Our hair needs a lot of care and attention. Hair gets greasy because **glands** under the skin produce oil. A small amount of this oil makes hair look healthy, but unwashed hair looks greasy and lank. Greasy hair will not only make you look and feel like something out of a science fiction film, but it can also make you spotty. Spots will form if the pores in your skin become clogged with grease.

CASE STUDY: DANDRUFF

Andy couldn't believe it when he started getting dandruff. His Dad had always had it and never did anything about it. It was so embarrassing – he would be wearing a dark suit or jumper and you could see all those bits of white flakes on his shoulders. Now Andy had the same problem. To makes matters worse he had been teasing that 'flaky head' Michael, who also had dandruff. Now he'd get it in the neck from his mates.

Dandruff – the facts

The white flakes of dandruff seen in some people's hair or even on their shoulders are actually flakes of dry, dead skin. The cause of dandruff is a dry scalp. People can easily treat their dandruff by washing their hair a couple of times a week with an anti-dandruff shampoo. These shampoos can be bought at all large stores and chemists. Perhaps Andy should also think twice before teasing someone.

Anti-dandruff shampoos can help restore the balance of oils in the scalp and stop large pieces of dry skin flaking off.

TIPS FOR GREAT HAIR

- Wash your hair regularly.
- Use specialized shampoo for greasy or dry hair, or for scalp problems such as dandruff.
- Brush or comb your hair daily.
- If your hair is greasy don't use conditioners with every wash.
- A regular cut or trim will keep your hair looking good.
- Wash your brush and comb on a regular basis.
- Plenty of fruit, vegetables and water in your diet will help keep your hair healthy.

It is worth making regular checks to see if you have dandruff – wear dark clothes before combing your hair, then check your shoulders for flakes of skin.

In the 1980s punks had a unique fashion style which often included elaborately spiked and coloured hairdos.

Colour coding

There are lots of exciting shades of hair dyes and bleaches available. But beware as many of these products contain high levels of peroxide or ammonia. These chemicals dry your hair out and cause split ends. There are many other products available which don't have such drastic side effects, such as semi-permanent colours that wash out over a couple of months. But before you choose a colour, remember that you have to go to school in the morning!

Check it out!

We can use our hair to say something about ourselves or to make a statement. For some people, this involves saying that they belong to a particular group of people or a religious group. Others may be making some kind of statement to society, for example in the 1970s and 80s punks and skinheads made very strong statements with their hair. This was a way of identifying themselves as a group who were unconventional, and even rebellious.

Exercise and rest

Why bother to exercise?

You may wonder whether exercise is really worth the time and effort it takes. Here are a few reasons why exercise is a good idea.

Exercise

- is an important part of taking care of your body
- is fun

Exercise and team work can make your mind more alert and your reaction times faster.

- strengthens muscles and maintains healthy bones
- keeps your body flexible
- is a good way of meeting people and making friends
- gets rid of pent-up emotions and anger and can lift your mood.

The type of exercise you choose can depend on a variety of things, such as access to, and the cost of joining a club, plus the cost of equipment. You will no doubt prefer certain sports, and may also be influenced by the views of your friends.

Choose a sport you enjoy doing and can keep up. Check up on the facilities available locally and consider the cost. There are many sports to choose from so try a few before deciding which one is right for you.

Warming up

If you are not used to exercise take it slowly at first – your body needs time to build up stamina. Gradually build up the amount of time you spend exercising, aiming for about half an hour at least three times a week. To avoid straining or pulling your muscles make sure you warm up before you start doing any exercise. Do a few simple stretches first.

EXERCISE TIPS
- When you have to walk somewhere, walk faster.
- Cycle or walk to school.
- Walk up stairs instead of taking a lift or escalator.
- Walk short distances rather than catching the bus or train.

Aerobic exercise

The most important muscles in your body are those of the heart. They work for 24 hours a day, every day, pumping blood around your body. Aerobic exercise, at least three times a week, helps to strengthen these vital muscles, keeping the heart healthy. Aerobic exercise is when you are exerting enough energy to make you out-of-breath, so that your heart has to work harder and increase its rhythm to maintain the blood-flow necessary to supply enough oxygen to the rest of your muscles.

Relaxation

Although exercise needs to be balanced with a good **diet**, sleep and relaxation are important, too. Give yourself time at the end of each day to relax. Avoid coming home from school and attacking your homework straight away, if possible. Working straight away may be the routine that best suits you, but you may feel fresher if you give yourself just half an hour to an hour relaxation time – watch television, read a book, go for a bike ride, have a kick around with a ball, clear your mind and have something to eat, before getting down to your school work. However, beware of watching too much television, and look out for the 'couch potato' syndrome. Once on, the TV can be difficult to turn off. Suddenly it can be very late and you have not even touched that work!

Sleep

A good night's sleep is important – it helps your body to recharge its batteries ready for the next day. People vary in how much sleep they need, but on average about eight hours is enough. If you wake up feeling tired, it probably means you haven't had enough sleep and will find it difficult to concentrate during the day. Again, the lure of that little box (the TV) can be difficult to resist. Late-night television viewers – beware!

Diet and nutrition

A balanced diet – why bother?

Your body needs food to grow, develop and function efficiently. A varied, well-balanced **diet** is enjoyable, will affect the way you look and feel, and is good for your general health.

Different foods contain different types of **nutrients**, each of which has a different function. You need the right balance of each of these to maintain a healthy body.

This is a 'healthy diet pyramid' which shows the foods we should eat regularly and the foods we should eat only occasionally.

Bread, breakfast cereals, pasta, rice and potatoes

All these contain **carbohydrates**, which supply us with slow-release energy. The wholemeal varieties are especially good sources of **fibre**, which is important for keeping the digestive system working properly, preventing constipation and reducing the risk of **cancer** in your large intestine. Wholemeal means they are less refined and therefore contain more nutrients than a white variety of rice or bread, for instance.

All the foods in this group also contain small amounts of valuable **vitamins**, **minerals** and **proteins**.

Fruit and vegetables

These supply us with vitamins and minerals, as well as fibre, and are important in the body's defence system. Eat as much fresh fruit and vegetables as possible every day – the recommended minimum is five pieces/portions.

fats, oils and sweets

milk, cheese and yoghurt

meat, fish, eggs, pulses and nuts

fruit

bread, cereals, pasta and rice

vegetables

12

Milk, cheese and yoghurt

These foods contain a wide variety of key nutrients such as protein, minerals and vitamins. They are a good source of the **element** calcium which is essential for the development of strong, healthy bones. A high intake of calcium in teenage years strengthens a young person's bones and can help prevent **osteoporosis**. Osteoporosis is a bone disease that is a particular problem for women in later life. A pint of milk a day will provide a good proportion of the daily requirements of calcium (choose full fat or semi-skimmed). If you really hate the taste or texture of milk, try milkshakes. You may be worried about your weight, but do not give up milk, instead avoid snacks rich in fat, such as chocolate bars and packets of crisps. If you are allergic to dairy products, try alternative sources of calcium, such as fish, oranges and leafy green vegetables.

Meat, fish, eggs, pulses and nuts

As well as being excellent sources of protein these also supply a wide variety of minerals and vitamins. You need protein for your body to build and repair body cells and tissue, and to produce **hormones** as well as other substances.

Lean cuts of meat, such as chicken (without the skin) or fish, are low in fat. Red meat and liver are great sources of iron, which is needed to prevent **anaemia** and will assist in replacing blood loss during a **period**. Pulses (green beans, lentils, peas and baked beans), green vegetables, wholegrain bread and eggs also contain some iron.

If you are a vegetarian, pulses and nuts combined with breads, cereals and potatoes will improve the protein value of your diet. Meals that include these are beans on toast and lentils with rice.

Butter, margarine and oils

These are all high in fat. You need only a small amount of these in your diet for good health. Too much can increase the risk of heart disease in later life, but small amounts are important to help the body absorb vitamins and to provide fuel for energy.

SOME OLD SAYINGS

'Breakfast is the most important meal of the day' – Your body needs a good start to the day and food helps to stimulate the brain. If you miss breakfast you will feel hungry later in the morning and will find it difficult to concentrate.

'You are what you eat' – This old saying is very true; a well-balanced diet will help you to stay fit and well, and contribute to your general well being.

'Thin is beautiful' – We are persuaded to believe this by the media. However, we are all different shapes and sizes – some of us are naturally thin while others have more rounded bodies. Most of us, both male and female, are not the shape and size of the models we see on our television screens or in magazines. What we see may not even be the model's true figure – computers and special photo techniques are sometimes used to manipulate what is shown.

Female and male bodies

Gender is determined the moment a sperm penetrates an **egg cell**. The first thing you may have heard when you were born was 'it's a boy' or 'it's a girl'.

The female body

Fallopian tubes

These tubes, which look rather like outstretched arms with finger ends, are about 10–12 centimetres long. The inside is no more than the diameter of a human hair. These tubes provide the pathway along which an egg cell, or **ovum**, will travel to the **uterus**. It is in these tubes that an egg cell and sperm will meet, and **fertilization** takes place.

Cervix

The **cervix** leads from the uterus to the **vagina**. Its opening is plugged with **mucus**, with only a small hole for blood to flow through during a **period**. During **ovulation** the mucus thins – allowing the sperm to enter the uterus.

Vulva

The **vulva** is the outside part of the female sexual organs, or genitalia. The vulva consists of two outer lips, or outer labia, on which the **pubic** hairs grow, and two inner, thinner lips, or inner labia. Between the labia are: the **clitoris** at the front, the **urethra** (exit for urine) in the middle and an opening to the vagina behind. Finally, the back opening is the **anus**.

Vagina

The vagina connects the uterus with the outside of the body. It is approximately 8 centimetres long, and it has ridged walls of muscle, which open during sexual intercourse and stretch in childbirth.

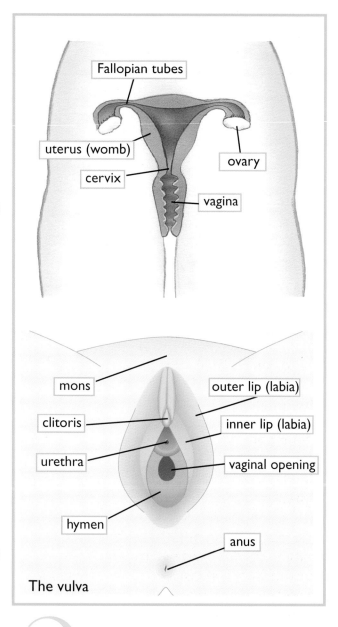

The vulva

The female reproductive organs.

Ovaries

At birth, the ovaries contain about 400,000 egg cells, or **ova**. From puberty, one ovum is released once a month. This travels down a Fallopian tube and into the uterus.

Uterus

The uterus, or womb, is pear-shaped and about the size of a clenched hand. The walls consist of a thick muscular tissue, which in pregnancy stretches to many times its normal size to hold the growing baby.

Clitoris

The two inner lips of the labia form a hood over the clitoris. The clitoris is similar to the male **penis**, but much smaller, although it is just as sensitive to touch.

Urethra

This is the opening from the bladder through which urine comes out.

Anus

The anus is the exit from the body for waste, and undigested food.

The male body

Penis and testes

The male reproductive organs, or genitals, are the penis and the **testes**, or testicles.

Erectile tissue

During erections, the erectile tissue of the penis fills with blood and becomes larger and harder.

Foreskin

This is a piece of skin that covers the tip of the penis. Some boys have their **foreskin** removed soon after birth in an operation known as circumcision. This is usually for religious reasons, or because it is then easier to keep clean. The foreskin needs to be rolled back and washed regularly, especially after puberty.

Sperm

The testes are oval in shape, sit in a sac of skin called the scrotum and hang either side of the penis. Inside each testis, there is a mass of tiny tubes where sperm are produced. Sperm are microscopic cells which, during sexual intercourse, are

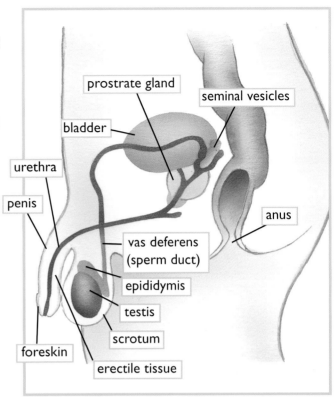

The male reproductive organs.

ejaculated into the woman's vagina and may fertilize her egg cell. Sperm travel from the testes to the **epididymis** where they mature. Then they travel to a larger tube called the **vas deferens**, or sperm duct. From here they move towards the penis, passing through **glands** called the **seminal vesicles** and the **prostrate gland**. Both these glands produce fluids which are added to the sperm to make a mixture called **semen**. Sometimes semen is stored in either the epididymis or in small parts of the seminal vesicles. Boys start producing sperm during puberty and can go on producing sperm throughout life.

Urethra

The vas deferens connects with the urethra (the exit from the bladder). Semen travels through the urethra and leaves the body through the tip of the penis.

Puberty

Puberty is the time when your body begins to change from a child's to that of a woman or a man. It starts at different times for males and females. Girls begin puberty between the ages of 10 and 12, although it can begin before or after this age. Boys tend to begin puberty between 13 and 15, but it could be earlier or later.

How does it all begin?

Puberty begins in a part of the brain called the **hypothalamus**. At puberty this starts to produce special substances called **stimulating hormones**. These hormones trigger the **pituitary gland**, which is also at the base of the brain. In both males and females this gland begins to produce higher levels of two stimulating hormones: FSH (follicle stimulating hormone) and LH (luteinizing hormone). These two hormones act as triggers to begin the whole process of puberty.

The female

At puberty, in response to FSH and LH, the **ovaries** start to mature the **egg cells**, or ova. The ovaries also begin to produce increased amounts of the hormones **oestrogen** and **progesterone**. These two hormones start the growth and development of a young girl's body into that of a young women. The four hormones, FSH, LH, oestrogen and progesterone, work together every month during the **menstrual cycle**, or **period**.

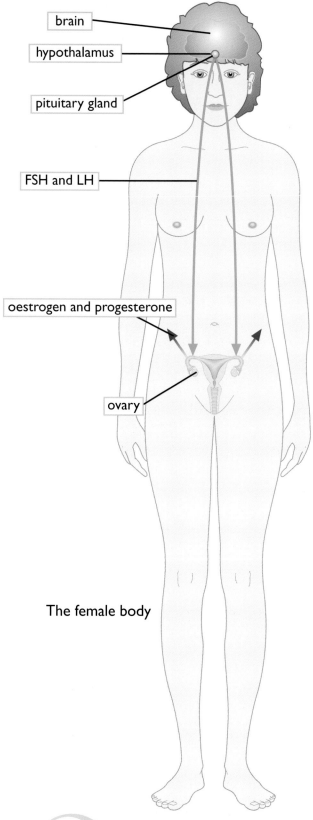

brain

hypothalamus

pituitary gland

FSH and LH

oestrogen and progesterone

ovary

The female body

Puberty is a big time of change, and hormones produced in the body trigger different parts of it to develop.

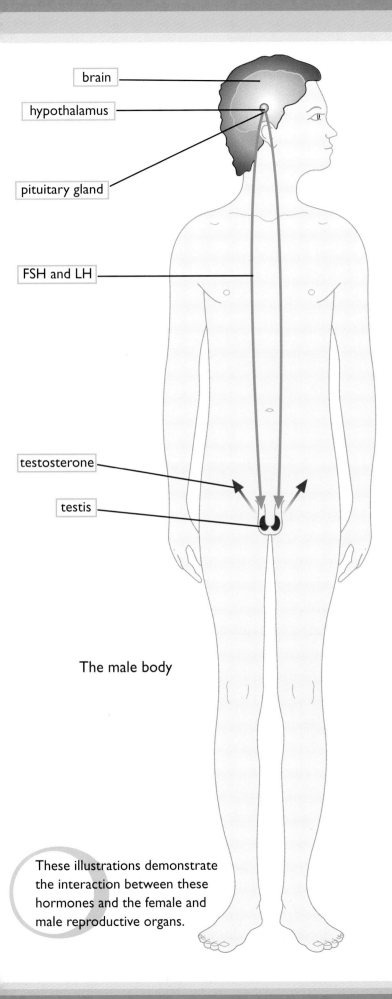

brain

hypothalamus

pituitary gland

FSH and LH

testosterone

testis

The male body

These illustrations demonstrate the interaction between these hormones and the female and male reproductive organs.

The male

Triggered by FSH and LH, the testes begin to produce **sperm**. They also start to produce their own hormone called **testosterone**, the hormone that begins the development of a young boy's body into that of a young man.

What are hormones?

Hormones are chemicals produced in our bodies. They make up a part of the body's communication system. Like a telephone network, they pass messages from one part of the body to another. They are produced by **endocrine glands**. The pituary gland is an example of an endocrine gland. There are many different types of hormones, not all of which are involved with puberty. For example, the hormone that has been causing your body to grow from a baby into a young person, is the growth hormone. You also have another hormone called adrenaline. When something or someone frightens you, adrenaline prepares your body to react – it makes you stand and fight, turn and run, or take the appropriate action.

Changing bodies

How are you shaping up?

This is the time when your body changes from a child's body to that of a young man or woman. Be careful during this time not to compare yourself too much with your friends – you may all be changing at different moments and speeds. One of the great things about human beings is that they come in all sorts of shapes and sizes, so none of us are the same.

Becoming a woman

Your body begins to change from that of a girl's to a young woman's at around the age of 10 or 11. However, it is perfectly normal if the changes occur earlier or later. You experience what is called a growth spurt, often growing taller than the boys in your class. Your breasts begin to develop; hairs grow under your armpits and on your **pubic** area; your thighs, and your hips and breasts become more rounded. It is during this time that your **periods** may begin. As your body changes, so will your feelings and attitudes.

FEMALE CHANGES AT PUBERTY

- Grow taller
- Facial skin secretes more oil
- Glands become more active and perspire more
- Hair begins to grow
- Breasts develop and **areolas** darken and become larger
- Hips and thighs widen out and become more developed and rounded
- Pubic hairs begin to grow

It is not just your body that changes at puberty. Your attitudes will change too and the opinions of your friends will be important to you.

Becoming a man

The changes occur over a period of time and happen to different people at different times. Don't worry if you are different to your friends – it is normal. To begin with your **testes** start to grow, the scrotum (the pouch of skin containing the testes) drops lower and becomes more wrinkly. The skin of the scrotum also changes, becoming either redder if you are fair, or darker if you are dark-skinned. Your **penis** also grows longer and thicker.

As you develop from a boy into a man your body changes in other ways, too – you grow taller, your shoulders widen and your muscles become stronger. You also grow hair in new places on your body, such as under your arms, on your chest and face and in the pubic area (the amount of hair depends on the genes you inherited from your parents). Your voice will deepen. At the same time you may find that your feelings and attitudes begin to change.

MALE CHANGES AT PUBERTY

- Grow taller
- Facial skin secretes more oil
- Glands become more active and perspire more
- May or may not have some hair growth
- Pubic hairs begin to grow

The menstrual cycle

The average menstrual cycle in women usually takes 28 days, but it can vary between 21 to 42 days.

Figure 1: Day 1 of the menstrual cycle –
- the thickened lining of the **uterus** is shed,
- the **pituitary gland** produces FSH and LH,
- these **hormones** stimulate an **egg cell** (**ovum**) to mature inside the **ovary** in a tiny sac called a **follicle**. (This is usually a different ovary from the previous month).

Figure 2: By about day 7 –
- the follicle is producing the hormone **oestrogen** which makes the lining of the uterus thicken,
- as the follicle matures it appears as a swelling on the surface of the ovary.

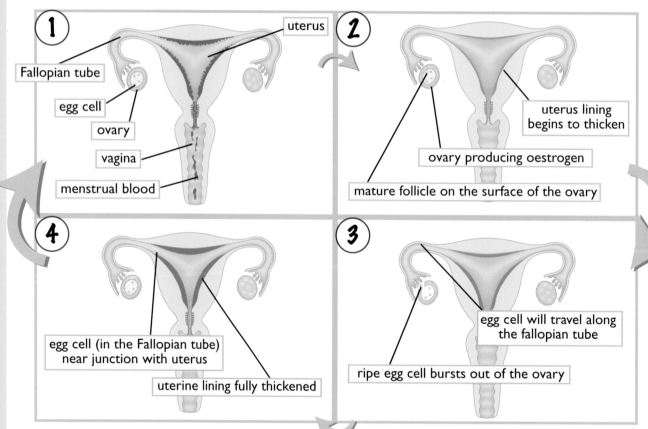

1
- uterus
- Fallopian tube
- egg cell
- ovary
- vagina
- menstrual blood

2
- uterus lining begins to thicken
- ovary producing oestrogen
- mature follicle on the surface of the ovary

4
- egg cell (in the Fallopian tube) near junction with uterus
- uterine lining fully thickened

3
- egg cell will travel along the fallopian tube
- ripe egg cell bursts out of the ovary

Figure 4: Days 18 to 28 –
- the egg cell makes its way down the Fallopian tube, towards the uterus. If during this journey a **sperm** does not fertilize the egg cell, the blood-rich lining of the uterus will not be needed,
- it disintegrates and a **period** begins,
- and the menstrual cycle starts all over again.

Figure 3: At about 12 to 16 days –
- the pituitary gland increases its production of LH. This causes the mature egg cell to burst out of the ovary,
- the empty follicle begins to produce the hormone **progesterone**,
- this hormone increases the flow of blood to the lining of the uterus in preparation for the arrival of a **fertilized** egg cell.

Sanitary bits and bobs

Sanitary towels or tampons are worn to absorb the blood lost during a period. You have probably seen lots of different brands and types in the supermarket, chemist or advertised in magazines.

Sanitary towels are pads of absorbent material, with one waterproof side. They come in a variety of shapes and sizes and are worn inside your pants. Towels should be changed every three to four hours, or more often if necessary. During the night it is best to use a larger, thicker towel.

Tampons are tight tubes of cotton wool with a string at one end. The string is used to pull the tampon out when it needs to be changed. As with towels, tampons need to be changed every three to four hours. They are available in different sizes, according to the rate of blood flow, and are inserted into the **vagina** where they absorb the flow of blood. You can get larger size tampons for the night-time. Some people worry that they may put a tampon into the wrong opening, such as the **anus** or **urethra**, but this would be very difficult to do as they are both very small and tight openings. Some people also worry that tampons may get stuck in the body, but it is very unlikely that this will happen. Some young girls feel more comfortable with towels for the first year or two of their periods. If your period begins at school, go to the school secretary or nurse as they will have a supply of sanitary towels.

Towels and tampons should not be disposed of down the toilet as this causes pollution in places such as beaches. Most toilets provide special bins and bags.

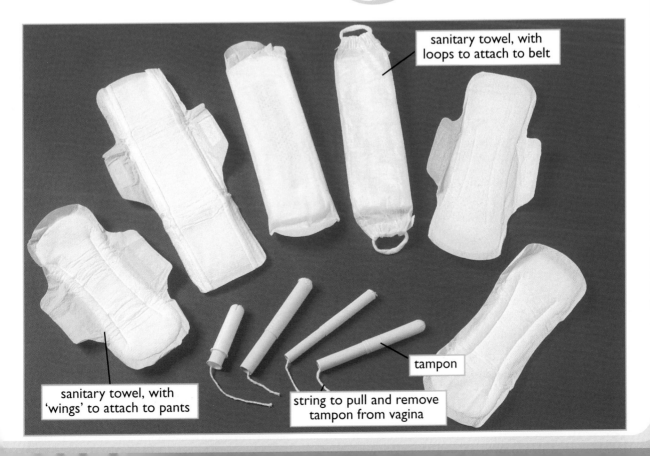

sanitary towel, with loops to attach to belt

tampon

sanitary towel, with 'wings' to attach to pants

string to pull and remove tampon from vagina

Any questions?

Many different things are happening to your body. You may want answers to all the questions in your head but are not sure who to ask, or where to get the information.

Periods

How often will your periods come?

On average every 28 days, but for some women it is every 22 and others up to every 43. But when you first start having **periods** they may not happen each month. Keep a record in your diary noting when your period begins and how long it lasts.

How much blood do you loose?

On average just a cupful of **menstrual flow** is lost. Only about 30 per cent of this is blood and it is soon replaced by the body. Menstrual flow also contains the thickened lining of the **uterus** called the **endometrium**.

What about period pains?

There are a number of ways to help relieve period pains.

- Exercise – try going for a long walk, take some deep breathes, or try some stretching exercises.
- Have warm drinks and food as they are more comforting than cold ones.
- A hot water bottle on your tummy is soothing.
- A warm bath will relieve cramp-like pains.
- If your period pains are really bad, ask a parent or guardian to buy some painkillers for you, or visit your doctor and ask about painkillers.
- Try to stay active – periods are a normal part of life and exercise will help them.

WET DREAMS

A nocturnal emission or **ejaculation** is often called a wet dream. Wet dreams are normal and nothing to worry about. It happens when a male ejaculates in his sleep without being aware of it. You may wake up with a wet patch on your pyjamas or sheets. It's a good idea to check out where the clean sheets are – you may prefer to change the bedding yourself.

Involuntary erections

Involuntary erections in males are perfectly normal and can happen for no apparent reason. Suddenly you are aware that your **penis** is erect. The erection will go of its own accord, although concentrating on something specific may help. The first time this happens can be worrying and embarrassing, especially if it is in public and possibly noticeable.

MASTURBATION

Your sexual organs (male penis and female **clitoris**) are very sensitive to touch. Touching and caressing them is called masturbation and can be very pleasant and satisfying. Masturbation itself is not wrong or harmful to your body, but if it becomes a habit or you feel uncomfortable about it then you may decide it is not right for you and take measures to stop. Not all girls and boys masturbate – some never try, some do it for a while and stop, while others may be against it because of their religious or moral beliefs or culture.

It helps to openly discuss your concerns and questions with friends you trust and respect, or a school counsellor.

Relationships and choices

Becoming your own person

Puberty is a time of great change, when your body and appearance, your likes, dislikes and emotions are all on the move. You are becoming a person in your own right, beginning to develop more clearly your own views, attitudes and values.

Mood swings

The changes going on in your body during puberty also affect your feelings. One minute you can feel great, happy and confident; the next minute something can happen which makes you feel that your world is about to end. These are called mood swings, they are perfectly normal and are caused by the **hormones** in your body.

Feeling low?

Feelings and emotions are important. Most of the time there will be very good reasons for feeling the way you do. Life is going well so you feel good, or you've had a bad day at school so you feel really low.

If those negative feelings don't seem to be going away, it may be a good idea to try talking to someone you trust and respect – perhaps a friend, parent, or other adult. Some schools have counsellors available to talk to in private. Sometimes friends are not the best people to look to for advice and guidance, there are occasions when it is more useful to talk to an adult with some experience of life and an objective point of view.

"I feel like I am on a roller-coaster sometimes; every day I seem to feel differently."

Families

You either love them or hate them, or you may even feel both love and hate at the same time!

Most families are supportive and fun. Parents and guardians clothe, house and feed us, although some may not be able to. They can also nag us to death, not understand, seem never to have enough time for us, or treat us like kids. Brothers and sisters can sometimes be annoying and a pain in the neck.

It is important to show your parents that you can be responsible. This isn't always easy but can be done if you take responsibility for making decisions, and are prepared to admit it if you get it wrong. Here are some helpful tips.

Favourite parents' nags

- Do your homework!
- Turn off the television!
- Turn your music down!
- Don't leave your dirty clothes everywhere!
- Who are you going out with?
- Where are you going?
- Be back on time!
- You can't go out dressed like that!
- You treat this place like a hotel!

Got to go now, see you later.

Thanks but no thanks. I've had enough to drink.

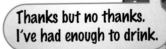

I'm sorry I know I shouldn't have done that, I was angry at having to be home so much earlier than my friends. Can we talk about changing my time to be in.

I was so worried and really angry, but I appreciate you saying sorry. Let's talk about it and come to some kind of compromise.

Friendships

Friends

How would you survive without them? They are there for you. They listen, make you feel wanted and valued, look out for you and are there when you need them.

Your parents' or guardians' view of your friends is not always as positive as you would like it to be. They complain that you spend far too much time with them. Often, they seem to not like some of your

Teenagers often spend hours sitting around and chatting with friends. Their emotions and interests are developing as well as their bodies.

friends – especially the ones you like most! At this time of change your friends can seem more important to you than your family.

But friendships can have their ups and downs.

Your decision?

Every day, you have to consider your likes and dislikes, what is important to you and what is not. You have to make choices about clothes, music, hobbies, films, and how you spend your leisure time. You may find yourself influenced by friends, family, advertisements, media comment and fashion. It is important to fit in with those around you, be like them and accepted by them. But as time goes by you will discover more for yourself from your successes and failures. It will be clear what your likes and dislikes are, who your real friends are and what things really matter to you.

QUESTIONS TO AN
Agony Aunt

QUESTION

I've had this friend since I was in primary school. We moved to secondary school together. We used to be so close. Now we seem to argue all the time, and she doesn't like any of the things I like. What has happened?

ANSWER

This can happen with friends. It sounds as if you have just grown apart as you have become older. There is nothing wrong with this. Perhaps it would be a good idea to talk with her, explain how you feel, start spending time with some other people at school and outside. You may find it is better when you spend less time together or you may find you just drift apart by finding different friends.

QUESTION

The other day Paul, one of my friends, told us he could get hold of some LSD for the party on Saturday. All the others seem really keen, but I'm not sure. To be honest, half of me wants to give it a try and the other half of me isn't really sure. If I say no, though, they will think I'm a coward.

ANSWER

It isn't easy when we find ourselves in situations like this. I can understand why you are unsure – it is a difficult decision to make. With any drug it is important to remember that you don't know how it will affect you. Friends may say it's great, which may have been true for them, but your body may react differently. Remember that you are breaking the law by having these drugs and if you get caught with them it could be very serious. Saying no to our friends is not always easy – but remember that if they are really worth knowing they will respect your decision to say no – even if they still go ahead. You may find, though, that some of your friends do not really want to take the drugs. Good luck!

Special relationships

That special friend

You may find yourself attracted to members of the opposite sex in new and different ways. You may change from thinking that members of the opposite sex are from a different planet to looking at them in a completely different way. You may have a special boy – or girlfriend who you want to spend most of your time with.

All these feelings are connected with sex **hormones**. These not only cause the changes in your body but also alter the way you think and feel about the opposite sex.

Going out together

You may enjoy spending your time with a group of boys and girls, getting to know them all. Gradually people in the group may start pairing off.

You may start to go out with someone and then discover that the person is not quite as you thought they were. You may decide to end the relationship. This can be very difficult and painful for both of you. It is not wrong to end such a relationship, but choose your time and methods carefully. Suddenly ignoring someone or going off with someone else, is unnecessarily hurtful.

During the teenage years you may have several special friends. You will discover more about relationships and how to get along with a variety of different types of people, including members of the opposite sex, family, teachers and relatives.

Crushes

You might find that you have a crush on someone you respect who is older, such as a teacher or senior pupil. This person may be a member of the same sex. This is perfectly normal. After a while you will probably find that this feeling stops and you will find yourself attracted to, and wanting to go out with, someone of the opposite sex.

Am I gay?

You may continue to feel attracted to people of the same sex as you, and so you may become unsure about your sexual orientation. You may feel that you are **gay** or **lesbian**. This can be confusing. It is important to find someone you trust and respect, who will help you talk about the thoughts and feelings you are having. Sometimes people who have these feelings are told to 'come out' which means telling friends and family that you are gay. But things are not so simple. With so much else happening in your life at present, it might be better to put off making such a decision until later.

There are many reasons why you may feel that you are gay, so try to share your thoughts with someone who you trust and who can help you to clarify your true feelings. The person should allow you space and time and help you to think about why you may be feeling this way. They should also be experienced in talking to young people about this type of issue and realize that you may be going through a confused period during which your sexual orientation is not clear.

Crushes on someone of the same or opposite sex are very normal. They may be with someone a little older or an adult such as a teacher.

Love or lust?

Media images

What is this thing called 'making love'? Is it just having sex with someone? Television, films and magazines show people jumping in and out of bed with each other and people having sex in all sorts of places. Films and television programmes show plenty of lust in action, but they do not always show the consequences of people's mistakes or the regrets people may have.

Lust features in film, television and magazines.

Making love!

Making love is different to just having sex. Making love is the physical expression of a special and loving relationship. Making love, or sexual intercourse, itself starts when the male **penis** is placed inside the female **vagina**, but sexual arousal builds up gradually as the couple kiss and touch each other. During sex the penis moves up and down inside the vagina, until eventually, at the peak of stimulation, the male has an orgasm when the **sperm** are **ejaculated** into the vagina. The female can also have an orgasm, but this may take a bit longer and is reached by the **clitoris** being stimulated. Making love is a very intimate act and a personal expression of feelings between two people.

Reasons to wait

- It is illegal to have sexual intercourse under the age of 16.
- There is always a risk of contracting a **sexually transmitted infection**. Some infections cannot be cured, although they can be treated – for example, **genital warts** and **HIV** (which leads to AIDS). **Clamydia**, which is a sexually transmitted infection, can result in **infertility** (difficulty in conceiving a baby) in many women and some men.
- A **condom** provides safer sex, not 100 per cent safe sex. Most teenage pregnancies happen when condoms split. So how safe is a condom? In fact it is 'only as safe the person using it'. When used during sexual intercourse, a condom is about 85 to 98 per cent safe.
- In the female the **cervix** is not fully mature until 17 to 19 years of age, and early sexual activity increases the risk of **cervical cancer** later in life. This type of cancer used to be only found in older women in their 40s and 50s, but now young women in their 20s and 30s are being affected by cervical cancer, too.
- You may have strong religious or moral values, which say sex outside of marriage is wrong and you want to stand by these.
- You may just not be ready and want to wait for that special person, someone to whom you feel very attracted and with whom you have a strong and committed relationship.

Remember:

- Not all young people have had sex. In fact the majority of young people under the age of 17 haven't.
- Think about it carefully and talk about it with someone you trust. This may be a parent, friend, or other adult you respect.

POINTS TO CONSIDER

- Sex is expressing physical self-surrender. It is saying 'I am totally yours'. Are you ready for this type of commitment?
- Is sexual intercourse the only way to express your love?
- Might you regret it?
- **Virginity** is something precious – have you really thought about whether you feel ready to lose it?
- Have you honestly shared and talked together about what it is you both really want?
- Will you respect your boyfriend or girlfriend if they say no?
- Has your boyfriend or girlfriend had sex with other people?
- How long has the relationship lasted, and how long will it last?
- Is your partner going to be faithful to you?
- Are you being influenced by peer pressure?
- You may have had sexual intercourse before you read this, have regretted it and now want to wait for that very special person. You do not have to have sex with every person you go out with.
- How would you cope with becoming pregnant or your girlfriend becoming pregnant?

Self-surrender is a big step for all of us and it is important to feel happy with the choices you make.

- If you have any doubts and/or feel unsure in any way, this probably means you are not ready yet.
- Even when you reach the legal age of consent you may not feel ready. Remember it is your body and an important decision you are making.
- Even if you have had a sexual relationship, you may not want to with your next boyfriend or girlfriend. It is your right to say no.
- Be very careful with alcohol; it often leads to saying yes to sex, when you mean no. It can also lead to not using a condom.
- Your body belongs to you and is very special. If anybody (someone of your own age, an adult or older young person, either of the opposite or same sex) asks you to do something or tries to touch you in any way you do not feel comfortable about or you know is wrong – it is right to say 'No!' and to tell someone.

Contraception

Contraception is used to stop a woman getting pregnant. It is also used to reduce the risk of contracting a **sexually transmitted infection** (STI). It is available from a variety of places, including **family planning clinics**, chemists and doctors' surgeries. Both men and women should take equal responsibility for contraception – it takes two to have sexual intercourse so it takes two to protect from an unplanned pregnancy and STIs.

Hormonal methods of contraception

These work by either stopping the **ovary** from releasing an **egg cell**, or ovum, or making the cervical **mucus** thick, preventing the sperm from entering into the **uterus** and fertilizing the egg cell.

The hormones can be taken by mouth (the pill), inserted under the skin in the arm or given by injection every few months. The most commonly used hormonal method is the pill.

Male and female condoms

This form of contraception is the most widely available. The male **condom** is made of thin rubber. It is rolled over the erect **penis** and works as a barrier, stopping the sperm entering the **vagina**. The female condom (femidon), is made of thin form of plastic and inserted into the vagina and so stops sperm passing through the

cervix. Both these types of contraception must be in place before the penis enters the vagina. They can only be used once and, in the case of the male condom, the penis must be removed from the vagina as soon as **ejaculation** has taken place.

The contraceptives shown here include the pill, condom (male and female), diaphragm, cap and IUD.

The condom can then be thrown away (not down the toilet as this adds to pollution).

The male condom is said to be 85 to 98 per cent effective, but it is really only this safe if used properly. Often for young people embarrassment and not knowing how to use a condom means that the condom may split or may not be put on the penis properly. Many teenage pregnancies are the result of condom failure. It is important to remember that a male can ejaculate some **sperm** (come) before he has an orgasm.

The phrase 'safe sex' is often used on the TV or in magazines; usually in relation to using a condom. Condom use provides 'safer sex' not 'safe sex'. Safe sex is when two people are in a committed, long-term or life-long relationship, such as marriage, and are faithful to one another. They have no risk of contracting an STI and are protecting themselves from the risk of pregnancy by using contraception.

Diaphragms and caps

These are inserted into the vagina prior to sex. They cover the **cervix** and prevent the sperm from entering into the uterus. They must be used with **spermicide jelly**, **foam** or cream, which kill sperm.

IUD

The intrauterine device, or IUD, is a small piece of plastic with copper wire wrapped around it. A doctor inserts the device into the uterus. It works by preventing the sperm and egg cell from meeting, or by preventing the fertilized egg cell from becoming embedded into the uterus wall.

IUS

The intrautarine system is a new device which is similar to an IUD, but also contains a slow-release dose of progestogen (artificially produced **progesterone**). It works in a similar way to an IUD but may also stop **ovulation** in some women. It is over 99% effective.

Sterilization

This is an operation that permanently prevents women from becoming pregnant or men from releasing sperm.

Natural family planning

To use this method a woman has to work out the days when she is fertile (likely to conceive a baby) each month and either avoid intercourse or use a barrier method during these days.

Emergency contraception

This is used when contraception fails, for example, a condom splits, or no contraception is used. It is available from doctor's surgeries, family planning, sexual health and Brook clinics, and from some hospital casualty departments. This method must be used within three days, or 72 hours. The earlier the first dose is taken the more effective this method is.

A second type of emergency contraception is to have an IUD fitted within five days of the unprotected sex. Both these types of contraception should not be used on a regular basis.

Sexually transmitted infections

Condoms and femidoms both offer some protection against STIs such as **clamydia** and **HIV**.

CASE STUDY 1: FAMILY PROBLEMS

Suzy's mother and her stepfather are going through a bad time at the moment. They are constantly arguing – there is usually a yelling match every night. Her little brother cannot cope with all that is going on. He sometimes comes into her room at night crying because he can't sleep. She feels as if she is having to cope with her little brother's feelings as well as her own.

All families go through difficult times, it can be very painful – you may feel unsure how to cope. You can feel torn between your two parents or committed to one and angry towards the other. For Suzy she has to be more like a mother than a big sister.

Most families have disagreements but adults should take time away from the children to discuss their views.

Handling difficult times and conflict is not easy and some of us find it harder to handle than others. Such times can be stressful, and stress can affect our health. Everyone goes through times when life is a challenge, so it is important to work out ways of coping. Finding out who you can go to for help and support is important.

It might help if Suzy talks to someone, perhaps at school, or there may be a youth counsellor available nearby. The telephone book or someone at the local youth club may be able to help with details. (Helplines are listed at the back of this book). This may help Suzy, but not solve the problems at home. It may help if her parents can find someone to talk to. Some parents find it difficult to talk to someone outside the situation about their problems. But it can often help.

I'll speak to you in any way I want to.

Stop shouting, it upsets Ben.

CASE STUDY 2: FAMILY PRESSURES

Simm feels as if everything is crashing in on him. His mother is putting so much pressure on him, especially since his father walked out and left his mother to take care of the family. She wants him to take 10 exams, but his teachers say it is too many. There is so much noise in the house – Simm can't find any space for studying. He isn't sleeping at night and is getting headaches most days. The exams are in two weeks but he won't be taking any if he isn't able to get down to work. He just wants to get away from it all.

Sometimes the expectations of our parents can be a great burden – they want us to do well, but it is more than we are able to deliver. This is a crucial time for Simm. Perhaps he should get the school and his mother together. The teachers could convince her that Simm would be more successful taking fewer exams. The study problem may be solved if he could work in the school library after school.

Bullying

Bullying happens in all schools. There are many different ways in which people bully:

- name calling
- excluding
- physical intimidation
- note-sending and gossiping
- racist and sexist comments.

Bullying, conflict at home and the pressure at exam time or just an overload of work can result in too much stress. Some stress can be helpful – it can make us get down to our work or help us to decide that enough is enough, for instance when someone is bullying us.

HOW TO HANDLE BULLYING

- Don't keep it to yourself – bullying is wrong. Telling someone about it is okay.
- Get help from teachers, parents and friends.
- Talk about it.
- Bystanders should intervene or get help – you are giving the bully permission to bully if you just stand there and do nothing, and it could be you next time.
- Bullies need to know it is wrong, but they may need help to stop.
- Work out ways of dealing with the bullying: ignore it, walk away, tell someone, don't react by hitting back – they may hit you back even harder!

Too much stress caused by an overload of work, or not being able to cope with a difficult situation can affect our health. It may cause us to become depressed, go off our food, affect our sleep or even turn to alcohol, cigarettes or other illegal drugs as a way or trying to deal with the stress or as a means just to forget.

It is important not to feel we have to try and cope alone. It is important to get help from friends, family, school or professionals, such as school counsellors or support services. There is a list of these at the end of this book.

STRESS – THE BODY'S RESPONSE

- headaches
- difficulty in sleeping
- poor appetite
- panic attacks
- depression
- turning to legal and illegal drugs
- anger and aggression.

Girlfriend or boyfriend problems

Relationships

CASE STUDY 1: UNPLANNED PREGNANCY

Vicky has missed her **period** and she thinks she is pregnant and has told Jason her boyfriend and her mother. She feels as if her world is falling apart around her. Her mother was angry and shocked, but has said she will go with her to the **family planning clinic** tomorrow to get a pregnancy test done and talk about what they are going to do.

What are the options open to Vicky and Jason?

- Go through with the pregnancy and have the baby fostered.
- Have the baby adopted.
- Keep the baby and bring it up themselves.
- Have an abortion.

None of these are easy options. Vicky and Jason are going to need to think them all through carefully. Some young people feel unable to tell their families. This is understandable but if possible it is better to tell them or at least tell an adult you trust. Another adult may be able to help you tell your family.

A school nurse, school counsellor, family doctor, family planning clinic or one of the organizations that help and advise young people are all there to offer support in this sort of situation.

CASE STUDY 2: MAKING LOVE

Paula is 14 and Marcus her boyfriend of just two months is 19. Up to last weekend everything had been great, but then Marcus had started to moan about only seeing Paula at the weekends. Last night they were at his flat and he wanted to 'go all the way' but Paula wants to wait until she is older. Marcus became very annoyed, saying he didn't know why he was going out with a school kid, and if she doesn't go all the way he will ditch her.

It can be difficult if you go out with an older person. They may have much more experience than you and expect more of the relationship than you are able or prepared to give. Paula may regret having sex out of fear of losing Marcus. If Marcus really cared about her would he put her under that sort of pressure? How would you handle a situation like this?

Coping with stress

Coping with difficult situations is very stressful. We may find ourselves unable to sleep, getting short-tempered with friends and family and flying off the handle.

Another way of looking at these sorts of difficulties is to focus on finding a way through, getting help from a friend, your family or an adult you respect and trust. It is at times like these that we learn a lot about ourselves and develop coping skills and strategies which will help in the future.

TIPS FOR HANDLING DIFFICULT SITUATIONS AND CONFLICT

Stand back and think about the situation.
- Are you doing anything to make it worse?
- How would you like it to be different?
- Can you actually change the situation?
- What would have to happen for things to be OK for you?
- Are your ideas realistic?
- Is there anyone who could help you – an adult or trusted friend?

Grief, change and bereavement

At some point everyone experiences some form of grief, change or bereavement. For some of you this may have happened very early in life. For others it will happen when you are older.

Bereavement means to be deprived of someone through death, but there are lots of others things which may cause us grief:

- separation or divorce of parents
- moving from/to a new school or house
- being hurt physically, sexually or emotionally by an adult or someone a little older than you
- becoming seriously ill, whether it is you or someone close to you, such as a parent or friend.
- **puberty** – saying goodbye to childhood and becoming a young adult
- bullying
- losing a pet
- events in other parts of the world (accidents, conflicts, cruelty, suffering, natural disasters).

When you lose someone you love, all sorts of feeling can wash over you – rather like large waves. You may feel out of control and overwhelmed. Feelings might include anger, disbelief and even guilt – somehow you might feel it was your fault. You can even find yourself thinking that if you went away the person you have lost might come back, or that somehow it could all be all right again. It can take time to work through all these different feelings. Talking to someone is likely to help you.

There are any number of stages in the process of grieving – from shock to the release of grief and acceptance of death.

CASE STUDY 1: DEATH OF A PARENT

Philip has lost his father recently. He died very suddenly.
 'It feels a bit like I am on a journey and there are different parts to the journey. I know that I will eventually look back and accept that yes, Dad is dead and I will never see him again. It will still make me sad, but it won't be quite like it is now. Some mornings I wake up and feel great – I've forgotten that he's gone. Then suddenly I remember and I feel sad and angry all at the same time. When he first died I used to throw things round my room and shout a lot. It isn't as bad as it was then, I just miss him so much.'

CASE STUDY 2: SEPARATION

Martin's parents recently split up and he feels responsible. He thinks that if he had behaved differently they would still be together. He is angry with his Dad and wants to talk to someone, but feels he should be able to work it out for himself. At school he just pretends everything is fine, he saw it all coming and, well, families do split up, don't they?

Pushing the feeling down and pretending that everything is fine does not work.

CASE STUDY 3: CHANGES

Jemima doesn't want to get rid of her teddies. She has had some of them since she was a baby. Her mother just doesn't understand. Her body may be growing up and she may look like a teenager, but she just wants to stay as a little girl. This growing up business is just happening too quickly. It only seems like yesterday that she was 'Daddy's little girl'. Now he does not give her cuddles in the same way, and both her mother and father expect her to act differently. Sometimes she wants to grow up and sometimes she wants it all to stop.

For some young people, going through puberty is like losing someone or something. The changes are too much, too soon. You may just want to stay being a child for a little while longer.

Coping with grief and change

We are all different and so respond in different ways to the pain of death, loss and change. There are a number of responses you may have.

'I can cope, I'm OK' – sometimes we feel we should be able to cope. We may feel we have to cope for others, our Mum or Dad, younger brother or sister. Sometimes people around are not helping when they say how well we are coping, when all we want to do is cry, get angry or just not cope!

Hitting out at others – this may feel good at the time and is understandable, but it can be difficult for others to cope with. Anger is natural and it is good to let it out. But depending on what you do with your anger, it can be dangerous for others or yourself.

Running away – you might try to escape from what has happened by pretending that nothing has happened or by actually running away.

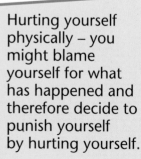

Withdrawing into yourself – it is good to be alone with your thoughts and feelings. But it may become a problem if you never want to be with other people.

Hurting yourself physically – you might blame yourself for what has happened and therefore decide to punish yourself by hurting yourself.

It takes a lot of courage to talk to someone about your feelings, but it usually helps clarify your thoughts and come to terms with your grief.

THINGS TO DO

To avoid reacting in a negative way try the following

- Talk to someone – find someone you feel safe with, trust and respect. This may be someone you know or a counsellor from the local youth agency or your school. Talking can help you accept what has happened, giving you the chance to sort out your feelings. It takes time to accept a death, your parents splitting up or the loss of a friend.

  Who you go to for help will depend on what has actually happened. At the back of the book there is a list of different names and addresses of various groups and organizations that can help.

- Learn a new skill – learning a new skill or practising one you already have may be helpful. For example, a musical instrument may provide a focus of attention and a distraction while assisting in the coping process.

- Exercise can help to get rid of feelings of anger or frustration.

- Write down your feelings in a poem, letter or diary.

- Allow yourself time and space to work out your thoughts and feelings.

- Don't expect to be able to cope alone. Reach out and try to talk to someone.

Rights and responsibilities

As you get older your health increasingly becomes your responsibility. Your parents may advise you or even nag you about certain habits or behaviour, but now more and more you are the one making the choices about your health.

Today we hear people talk a lot about their rights and this is important – but to have rights you also have to take responsibilities. For instance you have the right to a free education. Your responsibility is to work within your ability, behave in class, do your homework and contribute to the school community in a positive way – taking care of school property and not hindering the learning of other young people at school.

What are your health rights and responsibilities?

Your rights

- to be taken care of, fed and clothed by your parent(s) or guardian(s) until you are old enough to leave home
- health care and confidentiality from your doctor
- in Britain, free treatment from the National Health Service
- to be treated with respect at school and at home
- freedom from bullying.

Your responsibilities

- eat a well-balanced and healthy diet
- take regular exercise
- take responsibility for your own personal hygiene
- get enough sleep
- learn to take care of your medication if you have a prescription
- behave in a way which will not risk damage to your health
- visit your doctor and dentist, as and when is necessary
- value yourself and others, treating them with respect.

With your rights come responsibilities to both yourself and others. Some of your responsibilites are illustrated here.

Remember that taking care of your body is also about taking care of your mind and emotions. What you think and feel affect your health. There are many different types of people who are there to help and support you. Some you may have met and know about already, some you may not.

Family life

You may or may not feel close to your family. You may have a guardian, foster parents or live in a children's home, and not know your natural parents. Your relationship with your parents, guardian or carers may be difficult as you grow into adulthood and as they learn to allow you to make your own decisions and take up your responsibilities.

Sharing with parents, guardians, sisters, brothers or other relatives may be helpful and bring you closer, while at times it may be difficult and not feel right for you.

Friends

Some friends are good at giving advice, while others only say what they think you want to hear. Others may be good friends but cannot be trusted – in which case, don't share your intimate personal details or worries with them.

Family doctor

Your family doctor may have known you since you were a small child, so you may worry that they will treat you like a child. You may be able to choose to visit another doctor at the same surgery or may want, as you get older, to find your own doctor.

Some of you may feel comfortable with your doctor, he or she may be a good source of health advice. Many doctors today have a nurse who is also available to see.

School nurse

Not all schools have school nurses, but many do. Some school nurses run drop-in clinics at school or the health centre. Details of these should be available either at your school or through the local phone directory.

School counsellor

Some schools have a school counsellor; your form tutor or head of year will be able to tell you when and where she or he is available. There may be notices around the school advertising the service.

Specialist organizations

There are many types of these including youth counselling, family planning as well as local agencies to help with health concerns, drugs problems and family and personal worries. Agencies like these are usually advertised locally: your library should have details. Also, there are a number of useful addresses listed on page 46 of this book.

There are national charity lines such as Childline, Samaritans, Kidscape and the National Drugs Helpline. There are also groups that can support you if are learning to live with conditions such as asthma, epilepsy, diabetes, partial sight or hearing difficulties, etc.

Glossary

abortion the ending of a pregnancy. This can happen either as a miscarriage (spontaneous abortion) or when a pregnancy is ended on purpose.

AIDS (Acquired Immune Deficiency Syndrome) if you have AIDS, your body's immune system (white cells) stops working so that it cannot fight off infections. AIDS is caused by **HIV**.

anaemia a condition that occurs when the blood does not have enough red blood cells. It can make you feel tired and faint, and look pale.

anus the opening through which solid waste leaves the body when you go to the toilet

areola the area of skin that surrounds the nipple

bacteria minute organisms that can cause disease

barrier method a method of contraception that acts as a physical barrier, stopping sperm from coming into contact with an egg cell, or ovum.

cancer a disease that can effect different parts of our body. Smoking causes lung cancer.

carbohydrate a nutrient that gives your body energy

cervical cancer cancer of the cervix

cervix part of the female reproductive system, also known as the neck of the womb

clamydia a **sexually transmitted infection** that both males and females can get by having sexual intercourse with someone who is already infected

clitoris the most sensitive part of the female sex organs

condom a type of contraceptive

diet the food we eat – it can be either healthy or unhealthy

egg cells a female sex cell, another term for ovum

ejaculation a stream of semen spurting out of the end of a man's **penis** during orgasm

element a chemical substance that cannot be made into a simpler substance

endocrine gland a gland that produces a hormone into the blood stream

endometrium the lining of the **uterus**

epididymis part of the male reproductive organs

Fallopian tubes the tubes that provide the pathway along which an **egg cell** passes from the **ovary** to the **uterus**

family planning clinic a place where advice on contraceptives and supplies of contraceptives are available

fertilization the fusing of a female sex cell, or ovum, and male sex cell, or sperm. The ovum is fertilized by the sperm and a baby starts to develop.

fibre food that cannot be digested

follicle a collection of cells inside a woman's ovary, which contain an ovum

foreskin the piece of skin that covers the tip of a penis

FSH see **stimulating hormones**

gay sexually attracted to someone of the same sex

genes these are passed on to us by our mother and father. They determine our characteristics as individual people such as eye and hair colour, and whether we are short or tall.

genital warts a **sexually transmitted infection** that causes warts in the vagina and surrounding area

gland a part of the body that makes substances which the body needs to work properly.

HIV (Human Immunodeficiency Virus) the virus that causes **AIDS**

hypothalamus part of the brain, which produces hormones called **stimulating hormones**

infertility the inability to have a baby

lesbian a female who feels sexually attracted to other females

LH see **stimulating hormones**

menstrual flow the blood that is lost during menstruation (a period)

minerals a nutrient such as calcium or iron

moral values beliefs in what is right and wrong

mucus a thick sticky substance, which is found in several parts of the body including the cervix

nutrient a substance found in foods. Nutrients help our bodies to grow and develop.

oestrogen a hormone that begins the changes in a female body during puberty

osteoporosis a bone disease that can affect women in later life

ovary the organ where the egg cells, develop. A female has two ovaries, one on either side of her uterus.

ovum (plural: **ova**) a female sex cell, also known as an egg cell

ovulation the release of a mature egg cell

penis part of the male reproductive organs

period the menstrual flow of blood that a woman has once a month. It lasts for two to eight days

pituitary gland a gland situated at the base of the brain, which produces two hormones called FSH (follicle **stimulating hormone**) and LH (luteinizing hormone)

progesterone a hormone that begins the changes in a female body during puberty

prostrate gland part of the male reproductive system, which surrounds the male urethra

protein a nutrient that helps the body to grow, develop and heal itself when damaged

puberty the stage in life when a boy changes into a young man and a girl into a young woman

pubic describes the area of the body in the lower pelvis, between the legs

secrete to release something

semen a sticky, milky white fluid that is made up of sperm and seminal fluid, that comes from the prostrate gland

seminal vesicles small glands that produce seminal fluid (seminal fluid and sperm together make up semen)

sexually transmitted infection (STI) an infection that you can get by having sexual contact with an infected person

sperm the male sex cell

spermicide jelly/foam a substance that kills sperm

stimulating hormones two hormones called FSH (follicle stimulating hormone) and LH (luteinizing hormone). These two hormones act as triggers to the whole process of puberty, in both males and females.

testes part of the male reproductive organs

testosterone a hormone that begins the changes in a male body during puberty

urethra the opening from the bladder through which urine passes

uterus (also called the womb) the place where a growing baby develops inside of a woman

vagina the tube that connects the uterus with the outside of the body

vas deferens part of the male reproductive system. Sperm pass through the vas deferens on the way to the penis

virgin a male or female who has never had sexual intercourse

vitamin a nutrient that is important for the body's defence system

Contacts and helplines

BROOK ADVISORY CENTRES

233 Tottenham Court Road, London W1P 9AE
0171 580 2991 – Advice and help with any area of concern to young people on personal relationships.

CARE FOR LIFE

Pregnancy Crisis Centres
01256 477 300 – Advice, help, information and counselling in relation to pregnancy and abortion.

CHILDLINE

Royal Mail Building, Studd Street, London N10 QW
24 hour helpline **0800 1111** – Advice and help with issues related to bullying and child abuse

KIDSCAPE

152 Buckingham Palace Road, London SW1 9TR
0171 730 3300 – Advice and help with issues related to any kind of child abuse

HEALTH EDUCATION AUTHORITY

Hamilton House, Mabledon Place, London WC1H 9TX
0171 383 3833 – Information for all on health topics

NATIONAL COUNCIL FOR ONE PARENT FAMILIES

255 Kentish Town Road, London NW5 2LX
0171 267 1361 – Advice and information for single parent families

NATIONAL SELF-HARM NETWORK

c/o Survivors Speak Out, 34 Ornaburgh Street, London NW1 3ND
0171 916 5472 – Advice and support for self-harmers

NSPCC (National Society for the Prevention of Cruelty to Children)

National Centre, Curtain Road, London EC2A 3NH
Child Protection Helpline **0800 800500** – Advice and help with issues related to child abuse

PREGNANCY ADVISORY SERVICE

11-13 Charlotte Street, London W1P 1HD
0171 637 8962 – Advice and help in relation to pregnancy

SAMARITANS

If you just need to talk to someone, you can ring the Samaritans. Look in the telephone directory for your local Samaritans.

SPODA (Association to Aid the Sexual and Personal Relationships of People with a Disability)

286 Camden Road, London N7 OBJ
0171 607 8851 – Advice, information, support and counselling to young people with a disability

In Australia, use the following contacts:

AUSTRALIAN DEPARTMENT OF HEALTH AND AGED CARE

GPO Box 9848, Canberra City, ACT 2601
(02) 6289 1555
http://www.health.gov.au

KIDS HELPLINE

1800 551800 – Freecall for advice and support

REACH OUT

http://www.reachout.asu.au – Resource for young people going through tough times

SAVE THE CHILDREN, AUSTRALIA

PO Box 1281, Collingwood, VIC 3066

Further reading

Non Fiction

Adolescence
Nicholas Tucker
Wayland, *Human Development* series, 1990

Body Maintenence
Nicola Tucker
Health Education Authority, 1994

Child Abuse
Angela Park
Franklin Watts, 1988

Contemporary Moral Issues
Joe Jenkins
Heinemann, 1998

Disabled People
Peter White
Franklin Watts, 1988

Encyclopedia of Health
Marshall Cavendish, 1991

Keeping Fit
Paul Bennet
Belitha Press, 1997

Moods and Feelings
John Coleman
Wayland Press, 1990

My Body
Brian Moses
Wayland Press, 1995

Rights in the Home
E Haughton and P Clarke
Franklin Watts, 1997

The Human Body
Heather Amery and Jane Sagi
Reed International, *Discover Hidden Worlds* series, 1993

Too Old – Who Says – Our Ageing Generation
Violence in the Family
What are Children's Rights?
Craig Donnellan
Independence, *Issues for the Nineties* series, 1996

Young Oxford Book of The Human Body
David Glover
Oxford University Press, 1996

Index